Cascadia

Ann Lovejoy

Cascadia

INSPIRED GARDENING IN THE PACIFIC NORTHWEST

Photographs by Sandra Lee Reha

SASQUATCH BOOKS
SEATTLE

Contents

Introduction

In this region, the garden year extends readily. Structural, broad-leaved evergreens flourish in the mild climate, making a solid backdrop for a lavish assortment of early and late bloomers. The native flora is extravagant in variety, luxuriant in growth. Thousands of traditional favorite garden plants, edible and ornamental alike, thrive here. Best of all, the future is free. Ongoing and fascinating experimentation will lead us in new directions in garden design. New technology, new ideas, and a new relationship to plants and resources are all actively shaping emergent Northwestern styles. As our goals and principles take shape, our changing gardens reflect them.

THOUGH I HAVE LIVED and gardened all over the country, I came of age as a garden maker here in Cascadia. I arrived here in my early twenties, ardent with Green Revolution eco-concerns and discontent with conventional gardens. Here, where plants of all kinds flourish; here, where the mild climate allows active gardening all year round; here, where gardens spill into the woods and woods enter gardens, my developing taste and philosophy were formed. ❡ These days, widely as I travel, I rarely see gardens in other parts of the world that so closely approximate my inner vision of what a garden should be. Hospitable to the flow of daily life, welcoming to children and friends, pets and wildlife, Cascadia gardens are also enduringly beautiful. They are full of exciting plants in marvelous array, and they are full of life. Their greatest beauty lies in their enveloping flexibility, for the natural ways of the plants are accommodated as well as the needs of people. Now convivial, now festive, now peaceful retreats, our gardens celebrate all we value. ❡ Cascadia is the western Arcadia, pastoral yet magnificent. Framed between the Cascade Mountains and the Pacific Ocean, it stretches from southern British Columbia into Northern California. Though it is varied enough to include some twenty Sunset garden zones, all are lumped by U.S.D.A. hardiness maps into zones 8 and 9. ❡ If you have been gardening almost anywhere else in the country, welcome to paradise. Gardening here will provide you with a series of astonishingly pleasant surprises. Our mild winters and prolonged springs, gentle summers and lingering autumns make gardening exceptionally rewarding, as the following pages will prove.

What's Different About the

REGIONAL WEATHER PATTERNS create the most obvious differences between Cascadia gardens and those of, say, Boston, or Cincinnati. Several less concrete factors further influence the way people garden in the Northwest. Despite (or because of) still-abundant natural resources, there is a growing feeling that we want not only to preserve our treasures of water and wilderness but to make gardens that respect and refer to them as well. This desire has encouraged the rise of naturalistic gardens, a developing western specialty still in its youthful stages. The naturalistic garden encompasses uniquely western attitudes, emphasizing diversity of style and content, playing up regional strengths, envisioning what could be as well as what is. ¶ These attitudes— and the gardens—combine ingenuity and playful inventiveness with the comfortable absorption of whatever gifts of nature may already be in place. Native shrubs like Oregon grape (*Mahonia* spp.), salal (*Gaultheria shallon*), and flowering currant (*Ribes sanguineum*) mingle readily with Asian azaleas and English perennials. Rotting nurse logs shaggy with moss can nurture European ground orchids as happily as lady ferns and huckleberries. Farther south, chaparral blends excitingly with dryland plants of every description. ¶ The naturalistic garden is a clever and beautiful adaptation of natural patterns and plant community relationships. In these gardens, people and plants seem equally at home. Thanks in part to Asian design influences, Northwestern gardeners are especially good at evoking the natural. An opulent climate has made those in the southern parts of this territory remarkably good at creating adaptable gardens that are both meditative and places of sybaritic pleasure. In every case, their basis is not only beauty but refreshment, fostering the ancient, healing relationship between plants and people.

West?

The benign climate in this wet place supports plants in enormous variety, creating a garden palette of exceptional depth and sophistication. In favored microclimates, gardeners push the limits of hardiness, experimenting with borderline-tender exotica from Australia and New Zealand, South Africa and southern Asia. This one, *Brugmansia* 'Charles Grimaldi', is root-hardy to Seattle, blooming there in autumn. Potted brugmansias and related daturas will overwinter happily indoors, where their huge flowers fill the house with their jungle perfume. Literally intoxicating, the scent is strongest at night, when it creates a festively exhilarating ambience.

Mountains, Forest, Water, and Sky

NEWCOMERS TO THE PACIFIC Northwest are awestruck by the magnitude and multiplicities of its natural beauties. Snowy mountains loom at every hand, now hidden by clouds, now emerging in a dazzle of sudden sun. Deep forests dark with towering firs, hemlocks, and cedars are edged with graceful alders, lacy vine maples, and confectionery wild cherry. Northwestern roadsides are thick with cream bush and glossy Oregon grape, wild roses and salmonberries. The young woods are all but impenetrable, so dense is their undergrowth. Older woods are open and spare as a Zen garden, exhibiting Asiatic elegancies of moss and stone. ❧ Water is everywhere: ocean and lake, stream and cascade. The very air is saturated with it for much of the year. Fickle weather lends the sky new importance. We grow used to scanning the horizon and analyzing cloud patterns. The sky is huge here, as big as the west itself. Rarely plain blue, Northwestern skies are streaked, stippled, striated, feathered, and foaming with clouds, each promising its own sort of weather. The ever-altering climate is kindest to those who truly like weather in all its rich variety. Chances are good that a fine display of that variety will occur during any given day, any month of the year. ❧ Architectural homogenization has reached the region, yet wherever the natural persists, it dominates the work of man. Too grand to deny, such magnificence demands suitably big ideas in return; ditsiness doesn't cut it here. Northwestern gardeners must work to scale, employing emphatic design and powerful effects. Such boldness seldom looks overly obvious, for it is balanced by the subtlety of coloration, the shifting of light and shadow that hourly repaints gardens as well as woods and fields. The result is uniquely Cascadia gardens that bear the unmistakable stamp of their region.

Looming mountains and native trees create context for our gardens. This is most true in rural and suburban areas, yet many Northwestern cities enjoy spectacular views, perhaps encompassing several mountain ranges, with water on multiple sides. Where typical cityscapes are defined by apartments and offices, ours may be dominated by Mount Shasta, Mount Rainier, Mount Baker. Older neighborhoods are as apt to boast skyscraping Douglas firs and western red cedars as demure dogwoods or cloudy plums. These towering giants make visual and emotional links between the city and the forests that green the distance.

A Thousand Shades of Green

Dry Cascadia summers offer the perfect contrast to the sogginess of spring. Gardens echo this change in seasonally shifting greens, as the tender tints of spring mature to summer's darker shades. The concept is further expressed where lushness combines with the spare. In nature, ruddy madronas emerge like long-necked giraffes above thickets of Indian plum and salal. In the garden, tree trunks rise like living columns above a ruffled sea of greenery. Sleek or rough, their bark is marbled with mosses, subdued in summer, awakened to emerald brilliance by winter rains.

ONE OF THE FIRST THINGS people notice about the Northwest is the voluptuous smell of green. In damp woods or sunny meadow, sweet scents combine in distinctive, haunting fragrances unrivaled by anything artificial. The green itself—the sheer biomass of vegetable ecstasy—can be overwhelming to the uninitiated. Gardeners from elsewhere are seldom prepared for the intensity of growth that begins in February or March and continues, relentless, until the spring rains dwindle. The rush of green between March and April can produce true panic, the direct sense of the wild god himself that prickles the hair on our necks. Such exuberance of greenness, such extravagance of leaves and grasses leaping into being can dismay as well as delight. ℐ This spirit of natural excess clearly affects Cascadia garden design. From it come the generosity, the density of layering, the spilling over at the garden's edges. From it, too, comes the propensity for garden designs based as much on foliage as on flowers. The native flora itself provides a thousand greens in a hundred shapes; greens tinted with red and purple, blue and grey, bone and cream, and pale or dazzling gold. Add to this trove the hundreds of thousands of exotics one can grow here, and the possibilities expand indefinitely. ℐ Small wonder that so many regional gardens feature subtle and sumptuous orchestrations of leaves. Lapped and layered, varied in texture and tone, form and finish, leaves are both backbone and beginning for floral extravaganzas. The basic black of the garden, green is the greatest of garden neutrals, the color that enhances all it surrounds.

13

A Plea for the Trees

"HERE IN THE NORTHWEST," my local barista observed, "Relationships between neighbors are based on trees." People are drawn here by the expansiveness of forest and mountains and sky. When they build a new house, the first thing they do is clear-cut the property to let in the sunlight. The next thing they do is start reforesting, nearly always smack along their property line. ❧ Since trees grow at a great rate in these parts, before you know it, the neighbors' yard is half full of half trees that don't belong to them. Their lawns are invaded by roots, their houses are shaded, their views may be lost, but they can rarely do anything about it without starting a neighborhood battle. ❧ Even worse, the original lot still enjoys its view and sunshine. Such inequity makes for hard feelings. The solution, happily, is simple. Before planting trees, think long and hard about their future. Unless you live in a rural area, think small. Think apple, think bay laurel, think Irish juniper. ❧ Tree trauma can be avoided by intelligent action. Where mature trees spark neighborly difficulties, selective limbing can restore lost views and bring light to dark places. Selective thinning of clustered trees

will create a healthier environment for the survivors. Tree topping is never acceptable, for not only is it unspeakably ugly but the practice is very hard on the tree. It is far better to remove a troubled or troublesome tree entirely and replace it with a healthy, more appropriately sized substitute.

Although we come to the Northwest because we admire the lushness, many of us react to the overwhelming green by attempting to control it, to assert our human power over the forces of nature. Any gardener can tell you that this is a mistake. Just watch the way a lone daffodil or horsetail can push its blind way through layers of asphalt, splitting sidewalk or roadway asunder with soft green leaves.

Rather than pitting our strength against nature, we can benignly harness that green energy by making smart choices about what we plant. When we plant trees, native or not, we can select choice forms that won't outgrow their position. Instead of setting ourselves up for years of heavy pruning and damage control, we can enjoy watching our young trees develop, secure in the knowledge that what they do naturally is exactly what we want of them. That cooperative spirit makes for good neighbors, human and arboreal.

Framing a View

EXTRAORDINARY VIEWS CREATE visual extensions for thousands of gardens in this part of the world. Mountains and sea, lakes and rivers, rolling woodlands or gilded hills may all be glimpsed, if not readily admired, from garden and house. Overland or watery vistas on the grandest scale are complete in themselves. Such, however, are less common than sideways slivers of grandeur or mere peeps at majesty. Diminutive views may charm, but unless properly framed, they lack impact. ¶ To make the most of any view, but particularly of a minor one, the gardener must supply appropriate framing. Just as any picture gains definition and focus from the right frame, so too do garden views. Set off by slim junipers or sentinel yews, a distant mountain or a local tree is incorporated into the garden, just as a painting becomes part of a room. In each case, choosing just the right frame is critical to the final effect. The best frames are quietly attractive, showcasing the charms of whatever they embrace rather than drawing attention to themselves. ¶ A mediocre frame neither helps nor hampers, but the wrong frame diminishes its subject. When, for example, we catch the flash of sunlight playing upon water beyond a billowing border, we will appreciate that scene more wholeheartedly when the picture is framed by plants, trelliswork, or walls than when it is sandwiched between the neighbor's double-wide and a convenience store. ¶ Borrowed views need not be grand: a famous Italian one involves a minuscule view of Rome seen through the keyhole of the garden gate. Even neighborhoods without spectacular scenery may afford something charming or beautiful to be co-opted. Handsome trees that happen to belong to the neighbors, Victorian gingerbread, or even an aging brick wall might be used to decorate the greener walls of our own gardens.

Borrowed views can be made to appear far more exciting than they really are. Here, a modest side yard is elegantly framed with pillars and pots. Although not intended to be opened, the gate creates an impression of extension for the outer garden, a conceptual trick that works equally well with false doors or mirrored "windows" set into walls. Set off by the low fence and its handsome posts, the elderly apple tree within the yard is elevated to dowager status, while the area's main role as dog yard is appealingly disguised.

16

Water,

This is a region of rain. The falling water and the grey skies that herald its presence redefined light for regional artists, and for gardeners the pearly Northwestern light redefines color work. This watery light has a delightfully enriching quality, lending tender, subtle colors clarity and depth. Opalescent and soft, its mother-of-pearl luminosity is kind to cool, retiring colors yet tempers high, hot ones beautifully.

Water, Everywhere

In Cascadia, water is everywhere. Silvery days give way to gleaming, shiny nights under muted moons. Any given day may begin in shimmering mist. Low clouds come lumbering right into the garden, ghostly and dank. Even in high summer, heavy dew can spangle the grass until midday.

IF THIS REGION IS DEFINED by the solid forms of mountains and trees, it is equally a place of water. A long and wandering coastline makes Cascadia affluent in sea and sound, its long beaches complicated by countless inlets and islands. Inland, dozens of rivers are fed by innumerable tributaries. The mighty Columbia has scads of smaller sisters, some white with glacial milk, others brown with peat. Bogs, plain or peat, occur in soggy meadows throughout the region, and in countless gardens, water lies close beneath the earth's green skin. ❡ Though water is a constant, it is also constantly in flux. The sea surges with the tides. Lakes and ponds brim over in winter, then dwindle during the dry summers. Intermittent streams gush in full spate when the autumn rains begin, then die when the spring rains end. ❡ For much of the year, the air is alive with rain. Soft and insinuating, a delicate summer rain can seem too light to fall, simply filling the air like mist or fog, so you can work in the garden for hours without getting wet through. From October through April, the rain is steady and soaking, finding its chilly way down your neck no matter what manner of protection you devise. Rarely and most wonderfully, the rain pours in unbroken sheets from the sky, falling so thick and fast that the world shrinks to a pewter tunnel.

Water in the Garden

NOTHING IS MORE SOOTHING than the sound of water in the garden. When water moves, its shifting, sliding sounds celebrate flow and change. Oozing or dripping or pouring freely in cheerful cascades, water makes an ever-changing music. Where water sheets and tumbles into a holding pool, the garden is filled with its splash and trickle. Hearing that continuous lullaby, minds and bodies relax. So potent is the effect of water-sound on our psyche that it works on the smallest scale. In the tiniest garden, a basin set to catch the melodious drip from a narrow column can ease a weary spirit. A small bubbler turns a water jar only inches across into a recirculating fountain that sings like a running brook. ❧ The mere presence of water links the garden to the natural world. A simple birdbath attracts frogs and newts, dragonflies and

Thickly quilted with summer greenery, this handsome water basin has a year-round presence. In winter and spring, the gargoyle gushes and gurgles, its song loud in the quiet garden. In summer and fall, it drips and dribbles, its subtle music muted by the crowding water weeds. A ruffle of *Verbena* 'Homestead Purple' makes a visual lake around the basin, neatly reversing its role into that of a green island in a sea of ocean purple.

birds. In the garden, falling water blends with street noise, making it sound like more water. The human ear can be convinced to interpret traffic roar as wind or water quite easily, since those ancient sounds are more familiar to the unconscious mind than those of modern civilization. ❧ Water also captures light. Reflecting pools invite passing clouds into the garden. A plain water pot mirrors an unbroken circle of sky or a nightful of stars. Fountains sparkle and shimmer, spangling in sudden rainbows across leaf and bud. Moving or still, water has a fascinating, meditative quality, a quietude that pulls us powerfully inward.

The Absence of Water

Dry stream beds are traditional ornaments in Asian gardens. In Cascadia, such features can be both conceptual and practical, serving to channel the overflow of water during the wet season, evocative of cooling streams during the dry summers. They are especially useful on slopes and hillsides, where rushing rainwater can cut surprisingly deep channels overnight.

IT SEEMS IRONIC to speak of drought in this water-soaked land, yet drought is as recurring an event here as excess rain. Much of this territory enjoys a modified Mediterranean climate, its dry summers alternating with a long wet season extending from autumn through spring. Indeed, many areas receive little or no measurable rainfall between May or June and October. ¶ The regional interest in dry gardening and xeriscape techniques surprises visitors, who rarely realize how strongly summer droughts shape our gardens. Although the Northwest is often called "Little England" by envious visitors, the region's climate differs profoundly from England's. Most English gardeners don't own a hose. Here, watering cans are chiefly decorative and our sturdy hoses work overtime, since we have no steady summer rains to water for us. Summer droughts are news in England but a fact of life in the Northwest. ¶ Locals learn to select plants that tolerate wet feet when dormant yet thrive in dry soils when in bloom. We learn to group plants according to cultural needs, segregating summer moisture lovers where they can be easily tended. We seek out handsome drought-tolerant natives like Oregon grape (*Mahonia aquifolium*, *M. nervosa*) and cream bush (*Holodiscus discolor*) that don't require supplemental water, offering instead well-amended soils. We plant bulbs in beds of grit to improve soil drainage, apply generous mulches to conserve moisture, and give our gardens periodic deep soaks rather than frequent sprinkles. By suiting our plants to the climate, we get sturdily independent gardens.

23

Weather, Climate, Light

CASCADIA WEATHER IS MUTABLE, fickle, inconstant, and glorious, exactly like our gardens. Overall, the climate is moderate enough that gardeners can carry on all year long, adapting like our plants to the flow of weather. In an age when it is entirely possible to spend the majority of life indoors, insulated by cars and buildings and never needing to know what the weather is like, the continual connection with natural cycles is refreshing to the spirit. *¶* Newcomers often complain about relentless Northwestern rain, yet it quickly becomes an accepted necessity. Indeed, after just a week or two of dry weather, people talk dreamily about the rain. One gardener I know puts the sprinkler on the metal roof of her porch to produce the illusion of a soothing rain on hot summer evenings. *¶* Wind and fog are equally important climate modifiers in maritime gardens, particularly in the Bay area, where outlying towns can experience far more heat and sun than the city. All along the coast and inland along the Columbia Gorge, tidal winds influence garden temperatures even when the water is far from sight. Gardeners learn to moderate buffeting winds with hedges, fences, and screens, and seek out seaside plants that take fog in stride. *¶* Like Italy or Alaska, Cascadia has its own special light. What Northwestern painters affectionately call "oyster light" profoundly influences the regional palette of paint or plants. As in England, pastels look lustrous beneath our silvery skies. Dusky foliage and dark flowers smolder against glimmering greys and blues. Creamy colors that phosphoresce at twilight also glow on grey or wet days.

My favorite soil amendment is composted dairy manure. Light and fluffy, it quickly opens tight soils and helps keep sandy ones moist. In all my own gardens, this is the first amendment, and sometimes the only one needed to get started on garden making. All sorts of things can be used in place of manure, from spent hops to composted coffee grounds. The point is always to make poor dirt into rich soil. Beautiful dirt is a joy to gardener and plants alike.

Soils

THE NORTHWEST BOASTS an extraordinarily abundant native flora. Woods and meadows throughout the region are full of wondrous plants, from lowly mosses to looming Doug firs. Weeds and garden escapees like fennel and hollyhocks proliferate joyfully in empty city lots (or our own backyards). It seems obvious that a multitude of plants will grow here. However, there is a distinct difference between surviving and thriving. To successfully coax reliable, steady performances from our gardens, we need to give the local dirt a hand. ❧ West of the Cascades, native soils are usually acid. Most of us garden either on heavy clay that bakes to adobe in summer or on sandy soils that drain too fast for plant comfort. Frequent rains strip soils of humus and nutrients. Further difficulties arise in urban settings, where tired soils may be depleted of goodness. ❧ Even brand-new gardens may have fertility problems, for the ground is often scraped to hardpan during the house construction process. Though contractors may add topsoil, hardpan hosts no worms. Without worms to do the mixing, that new soil remains layered like chocolate icing on a sand-colored cake. ❧ Whatever the trouble, the remedy is nearly always the same. Whether our soils are acid or base, clay or sand, just tired or downright barren, nothing will improve their tilth, texture, and productivity more than organic soil amendments. Earthy substances like aged manure and compost add invaluable humus, the organic portion of soil that is the equivalent of vitamins for dirt. Without its nutritional boost, soil biota can't flourish, and though many plants may grow, only a relative handful will actively thrive.

27

Compost

Constantly flushed by rains, our regional soils tend to be low in humus. Compost not only replaces humus but opens tight clay soils, promoting better air flow to plant roots and improving drainage. In sandy soils, frequent and generous applications of compost help retain moisture and nutrients that are otherwise quickly washed away. In both cases, as the tilth of the soil is improved, plants become healthier and more vigorous.

BASIC GARDEN SKILLS such as making compost remain much the same the world over, yet regional quirks must always be considered. As anywhere, composts here tend to be neutral in pH, but gardeners who routinely add spent soil to their bins or piles often find their end product to be noticeably acid. Generally, our intention is to neutralize naturally acid soils with buffering compost to make the widest possible variety of plants comfortable. This is best accomplished through regular additions of horticultural lime (never the slaked kind, which is for outhouse use), which sweeten the compost considerably. ❧ Since our gardens tend to be in active use all year long, aesthetic concerns are important. Rough, half-finished compost can always be heaped on the vegetable patch in fall, letting the winter rains soak its goodness into the soil. In the ornamental parts of the garden, however, unsightly lumps of raw compost look out of place. In winter, when gardens need all the help we can offer, looks matter. Indeed, we should be especially conscientious about garden grooming during the off-seasons. ❧ In the Northwest, a day in January can be as mild as one in June (a fact that says rather less for June than for January, but never mind). We seize every opportunity to do a bit of weeding or enjoy a cup of tea in the wintry garden, basking in the mild sunshine. When we do so, we want to admire our gardens freely, not avert our eyes from their half-dressed state. Winter bloomers

look far more prepossessing when handsomely blanketed with finished compost. ❧ Compost mulches also feed hungry roots, which grow rapidly during winter thaws, and protect tender crowns from hard frosts. Though low in nutrients itself, compost makes soil nutrients more readily available to plants as it decomposes. An excellent top dressing, it can be used lavishly without concern for overfeeding, for, unlike commercial fertilizers, it will never burn young plants.

Garden Grooming

WISE WOMEN CLAIM the best manure is the farmer's boot. In the garden, nothing encourages the health and good looks of our plants like the gardener's hand. Light but frequent grooming gives gardens an air of well-being. Carefully tended gardens keep their freshness longer, lasting in power and beauty well into autumn, if not clear through the winter. ❡ As we remove tired foliage and spent flowerheads, all kinds of information passes unconsciously through our fingers. Looking more closely, we see that one plant seems crowded, another may have root problems, a third will need thinning soon. Quickly resolved, small problems stay small. Grooming is as much about appearances as health, yet it should never become prissy. Gardens where no imperfection is tolerated feel overcontrolled and uncomfortable. Well-groomed gardens are welcoming, with the contented look shared by all that knows itself loved. ❡ This constant if minor maintenance is the garden equivalent of brushing hair and cleaning shoes. When we tidy, now redirecting a wandering vine, now tying back a flopping clump, these little adjustments lend polish to our artful arrangements. Performed daily, grooming takes just minutes. Done weekly, the job may require a few hours. In either case, the process fosters an interactive relationship, linking people to the progress of the seasons, restorative for garden and gardener alike.

The Four Tiers of Nature

Visitors to the Bellevue Botanical Garden on Wilburton Hill will see nature's tiers enchantingly expressed in the extensive mixed borders planted and maintained by the Northwest Perennial Alliance. Intended as a showcase for perennials, the borders encompass plants of all descriptions (some ten thousand of them, at last count). The artful blends of ornamental small trees and handsome, multiseason shrubs create a complex garden context. Within it, thousands of perennials happily make their homes amongst a range of ecological niches.

CASCADIA GARDENERS ARE increasingly apt to create naturalistic gardens that echo natural relationships and patterns. When gardeners look to the native woods for lessons, they discover plants growing in a classic relationship best understood in terms of the four tiers of nature. In ecosystems as varied as the deep Alaskan woods or the golden hills of California, similar planting principles apply. Everywhere, trees shelter shrubs, which are in turn underplanted with perennials. Beneath these are ground covers, often laced with bulbs. Through the whole community, vines scramble upward, linking the lowest levels to the highest. The kind and quantity vary, of course. In Northern California, the madrona chaparral is far more open than the dense rain forests of coastal Oregon, Washington, and British Columbia. Airy or impenetrable, all Cascadia woodlands display variations of the four-tier theme. ❧ The concept translates excitingly into garden terms, where it proves exceptionally adaptable. In the smallest spaces, columnar trees and compact shrubs may be woven into tapestry hedges. Whether formal or casual in design, such hedges define the perimeters of the property and form the backdrop for artfully mixed borders. Reduced in scale, these miniature communities faithfully repeat the four tiers of nature, creating a comforting echo of the natural even in the city.

Natural Planting Patterns

NATURAL PLANT COMMUNITIES offer invaluable lessons for gardeners. In mountain meadows, on sandy beaches, in deep woods, plants are so generously combined that bare earth is rare. Generally, numerous species are knit together into flowery tapestries. In nature, monocultures like rose ghettos or heather collections are uncommon, even in the challenging serpentine soils that support a relative handful of plants. ❧ In the wild, plants appear in steady sequence. Early bloomers shine and fade, giving way to later arrivals whose burgeoning growth hides aging foliage. Natural sandwich communities arise in which several seasons' worth of plants share ground companionably. Nutritional needs fluctuate with annual growth patterns, and withering remains make natural compost, so there is always enough to go around. ❧ The patterns of nature are repeated in naturalistic garden borders, where overlapping waves of plants reflect nature's abundance. Most plants are communal, growing best in good company. Humans also thrive in the company of plants: many studies demonstrate that people who merely view greenery daily enjoy better health, lower stress, and a greater sense of well-being than those whose environment is entirely artificial. ❧ Evoking the natural benefits plants as well. Though many plants are site-adaptive, most grow best in appropriate settings and situations. When we recognize the microclimates and variations of ecosystem within our gardens, we broaden the available range of planting conditions. By carefully matching plants to situation, we can create happy communities that need surprisingly little supervision.

Oregon beach grasses shine in tangled majesty at summer's end. Bleached and gilded, their spangled seed-heads recall harvest richness and the long winter slumber to come. In autumn, the distraction of color removed, we can more easily interpret the patterns within this tightly interconnected planting. Though it is closely spaced, the shape of each component is apparent. In the garden, we re-create this effect by placing plants to emphasize their natural attributes. Grouped with mutually supportive companions, their strengths are bolstered, their weaknesses minimized.

Influential

Northwestern Styles

When we begin developing a personal garden style, the issue of control looms large. Ideally, gardening is a cooperative venture; the better we know our plants, the better we can assign their placement and the less intervention they will require. Discipline in both planning and planting keeps unrelated details from cluttering up our designs or obscuring our intentions. However, control can become so central an influence that little life remains. Gardens where chilly perfection reigns cannot make us welcome. The best gardens are not horticultural shrines to good taste but nurturing environments for people and plants alike.

EVER SINCE THE WAGONS rolled West, people have been drawn in increasing numbers to this exceptional region. Each wave of immigrants arrived with ideas about what a garden should look like, and each in turn was influenced by the land, its flora, and its climate. England and New England, Europe and Scandinavia, China and Japan, all contributed to Cascadia's own developing forms, not only garden making but architecture and art, literature and cuisine. ¶ Early gardens were mostly practical—typical settlers' collections of edible and medicinal plants brightened by a precious handful of ornamentals. There wasn't much room for plants in crowded wagons or ships' holds, and only the tough survived the long journey. Seeds, bulbs, and roots, slips and cuttings were carefully nursed. Once successfully transplanted, pieces of grannie's lilac and mother's peony were generously shared. To this day, older urban neighborhoods are filled with roses and iris that date back to the pioneer days. ¶ The timber boom brought financial success and its trappings, including formal gardens and parks based largely on English and European models. Asian immigrants made gardens that reflected very different traditions and aroused great interest throughout the region, beginning the process of fusion that led to Pacific Rim and naturalistic gardens. Visiting master garden makers from Japan and China created notable public gardens as well, among them the Japanese tea gardens in Seattle and Portland and the traditional Chinese garden dedicated to Dr. Sun Yat-Sen in Vancouver, British Columbia.

Asian Influences

BUDDHIST SAND GARDENS are perhaps the ultimate in refinement, having been honed to bare essentials over several thousand years. Winter or summer, little in them alters but the shifting shadows that spill over raked gravel and wrinkled velvet moss. It's easy to see them as stark at first, yet their history imbues them with both drama and romance. Their origins lie deep in the past, when an animistic society saw a world heavily populated with gods and demons. The *niwa*, or open space, of a Zen sand garden creates a circle of protection, making safe haven for gods and humans alike. White gravel or sand represents purity, while naturally shaped, uncut stones offer visiting gods a comfortable resting place. Evergreen trees, with their strong *chi*, or life force, may entice benign spirits to dwell within them all year round, blessing the garden with their presence. In preserving these forms, we can rediscover the dignity and serenity of their ancient originals. ❧ Pacific Rim gardens are natural hybrids, combining traditional Asian garden forms with the fuller plant palette of the West. Like formal European gardens, they are framed with woody evergreens, but as in Asian gardens, each plant is placed sculpturally. Evergreens and moss, gravel and stones are constant elements, yet their placement and partners are often quirky rather than traditional. Like green sonnets, these gardens are strict in form yet flexible in scope and interpretation. In winter, they are spare and contemplative, a study in line and silhouette. By March or April, azaleas and rhododendrons are bright with bloom, the maples hung with ruby or shrimp-pink florets. In summer, these gardens are meditative havens, subtle in color and sumptuous in texture and detail. Autumn awakens the latent fire in maple and azalea, their blaze reflected in water as well as the foliar jewels that spangle austere gravel and muted moss alike.

English Gardens

THE ITALIAN GARDEN at Royal Roads Military College near Victoria, British Columbia, is an excellent example of the way in which English garden styles were absorbed and transformed in the New World. Far more English than Italianate, this garden combines strong architectural elements with both formal and informal planting patterns. Vines romp through banisters and columns, softening the hard lines of the stonework. Nearby, geometrically arranged herb gardens contrast with billowy borders planted in the loose, romantic manner pioneered at Sissinghurst, where natural plant forms and habits are played off against structural hedges and flat lawns. Although formal English gardens had a profound effect on early garden design in the west, mixed borders and careful colorist orchestrations are more influential today.

Here, piquancy comes from the contrast between the contrived and the natural. Living limbs, sinuously interwoven, repeat the curving lines of the gate. Native alders are easily pleached this way, as are garden trees like laburnums, apples, and pears. Supported by rubber-coated wire, supple young branches can be braided or trained in patterns.

Main Street

Many experienced gardeners make it a point to plant short-stemmed flowers like sweet alyssum and rock roses (*Cistus* spp.) in their front gardens. "They are harder to pick, so they don't all disappear in the night," explained one earthy old gal whose Seattle streetside garden held something colorful every day of the year. "I grow lilies and roses and peonies in the back garden, or I'd lose them all," she said, adding with a grin, "That's where I grow those opium poppies, too: I used to have them all over the front, but the vice squad came and rooted them all out. I was furious, but at least those big lugs didn't think to look out back—there's twice as many of 'em back there!"

American

SIDEWALK GARDENS are my favorite kind, for in them we share our floral passion with the world. If few front gardens vary from the strict patterns laid out in some lost year in a faraway eastern city, there are always enchanting exceptions to that rule. In nearly every Cascadia neighborhood, that sterile pattern is broken by quirky, personal expressions of delight. Here, an ebullient garden bursts loose from its yard and tumbles down the street, filling parking strips and traffic circles along the way. There, a collector's treasure trove spills onto the sidewalk, offering everyone an invitation to see and smell sequences of fragrant flowers and handsome foliage. *¶* In my tiny, open Seattle yard, gardening became a communal experience. I got exceptional quantities of advice and commentary from neighbors and passersby, who loved watching the garden change over time. Most people simply enjoyed looking, but a few wanted to share plants and ideas. A handful even gave some time, weeding along beside me for a few minutes on their way home from work.

If Main Street gardens are a gift to the whole neighborhood, they often receive all sorts of gifts in return. In my Seattle garden, a pot of lilies appeared with a note explaining that the owner lived in an apartment and wanted the flowers to be out where more people could enjoy them. Another time, several sacks of manure arrived with a card saying, "For the roses." Over the years, dozens of plants were donated, from fabulous dahlias to a heritage hellebore handed down through several generations.

43

California Neutral and Tropicalismo

TEN YEARS AGO, the California Neutral school was utterly influential throughout our region. Stylized and determinedly tasteful, its gardens featured lots of hardscape: decks and patios, fire pits and barbecues, terraces and walls were extremely well represented. Relatively few plants were used, and most of them were tightly sheared evergreens clipped into living lozenges, or the kind of well-behaved plant that changes very little in size or shape over the course of its life. Where there were flowers, they were obviously chosen for their bloom-to-dollar ratio values. Strategically placed containers held relentlessly long-blooming annuals, which were arranged either in hot, hard colors or in lumps of timid pastels. Determinedly low maintenance, such gardens encouraged outdoor living all right. However, to plant lovers, they seemed bland, sterile, and decidedly boring. ❧ As a fascinating palette of semi-tropical plants from New Zealand, Australia, Asia, and South Africa became widely available, artful gardeners enthusiastically embraced the implicit possibilities. Just as the earthy salsas and sambas of South America begat musical tropicalismo, these gaudy, gorgeous plants inspired a sensual, stimulating, new kind of gardening. ❧ Daring, playful, exploratory, and excitingly beautiful, garden tropicalismo delights in exotic foliage and enormous, flagrant flowers. Gardens inspired by this school revel in the interplay of plant color, form, and texture, triumphantly celebrating the ever-altering flow of seasonal change as much as the fabulous plants themselves.

The sleek emptiness of California Neutral gardens appeals to those who dislike clutter. However, unless the wide expanses are amplified with varied and well-structured plantings, they feel barren and uninviting. In compelling contrast, the lush abundance of tropicalismo evokes a strong sense of intimacy with the natural world. In this stunningly beautiful sidewalk garden, what looks like gay abandon is actually a well-controlled melange of plants with compatible needs. Walking beneath the arching canopy, we are instantly transported to an enchanted forest or archetypal jungle.

44

Northwest Naturalistic

THIS EMERGING SCHOOL is so flexible that its gardens vary tremendously in form and flavor. Many, however, combine a collector's love of plants with an ecologist's appreciation for the native flora. Wherever gardens overlap with native plantings, the first principle is to assess what's already on site before calling in the bulldozers. Native shrubs like salal (*Gaultheria shallon*), Oregon grape (*Mahonia* spp.), huckleberry (*Vaccinium* spp.), and flowering currant (*Ribes sanguineum*) are highly regarded in England, but don't get much respect closer to home. Before rejecting natives in favor of exotic imports, reevaluate them for year-round good looks, strength of form, and graceful line. Cleaned up and judiciously pruned, many natives rival anything the garden center offers for beauty, and the price is right. ❡ Established natives also provide instant structural support. Big shrubs firmly anchor swirling seas of perennials. Mature trees make living columns as architectural as anything artificial. If bare trunks look too stark, let climbing roses, creamy native *Clematis ligusticifolia*, or rampant honeysuckles soften their lines and integrate them with the garden proper. (To encourage plants skyward, drape those trunks with black plastic pea netting. Nearly invisible, it allows almost anything to scramble up through it.). ❡ Casual or elegant, naturalistic gardens look appropriate in a multiplicity of settings. They make splendid transitions between woodlands and suburbs. In the city, even tiny naturalistic gardens create a feeling of connection to the natural world that overcomes concrete and asphalt. Still developing, this young style offers garden makers an opportunity to help shape its future.

Most naturalistic gardens are modeled on woodlands. While sunny parts of these gardens may be boldly brilliant, color schemes in shaded areas tend to be muted. Preference is given to quietly colored flowers and variegated foliage in cream and white, soft yellows and chartreuse. Their gentle glow brightens the deep or dappled shade beneath mature trees without startling the eye. Carefully grouped, showily ornamental plants like astilbes or coleus lead the eye naturally toward more formal or contrived parts of the garden, while subtler ones like bear's breeches (*Acanthus* spp.) and coral bells (*Heuchera* spp.) make the transition to native plantings visually convincing.

Working with the Wild

CASCADIA GARDENERS often face the challenge of creating attractive transitions between their gardens and the wild, which may mean woods or meadows, bluffs or beaches. To make such intermediate areas convincing, we must work with the wild, echoing natural planting patterns and incorporating a good percentage of native plants into our designs. Most gardens are more ornamental and formal near the house, growing wilder and less obviously controlled as they approach natural plantings. The points of overlap, where native and garden plants combine, are the trickiest to pull off. Naturalistic but gardenly arrangements work best, based on designs that play off line and form more than color. ❡ In woodland gardens, for instance, we might combine striped hostas and bold rodgersias, fine-textured grasses and lacy ferns, using several plants of each variety. Against the backdrop of the woods, simple, rather sculptural plantings look more at home than fussy ones. Select plants with clean lines, remove anything that looks cluttered, allow each plant room to show its natural shape, and your garden will ease seamlessly into the woods.

49

Editing the Woods

WHERE GARDENS ARE to wed woodlands, thoughtful editing of transitional areas is imperative. Simple yet amazingly effective, the process produces attractive Japanesque results very quickly. To discover what you've got to work with, start by removing all deadwood from the forest floor. Try not to disturb the mosses and ferns, and leave in place any large logs that have developed thick mossy coats. ❦ Next, lightly prune native evergreens like huckleberry, salal, and Oregon grape. Remove dead, damaged, or awkward stems, cutting back to healthy foliage. The goal here is not a rigidly controlled look, so once a shrub's graceful natural shape is revealed, stop. If you are lucky enough to find tree stumps sprouting huckleberries, or rotting nurse logs covered with lady ferns, treasure them as natural sculpture. Tidy them gently, but don't remove the shaggy mosses and mushrooms that are such a part of their charm. ❦ The browned fronds at the base of the big sword ferns should be cut off, along with any upright fronds that show winter damage. Remove anything unsightly from the forest floor, but leave the thick carpet of crumbly duff in place—this is nature's compost, an excellent growth medium for trilliums and other wild flowers. ❦ Big, healthy deciduous shrubs like cream bush and Indian plum (*Oemleria cerasiformis*) can be groomed in the same way. Where too many young ones are crowded together, thin the majority (or all, if choicer things are obscured by them), leaving only the best. Finally, snap as many dead lower branches as you can reach (use a ladder if you can) from the biggest trees, leaving the smallest possible stub. ❦ What you have left is nearly always a masterpiece of understated beauty, a natural garden that rivals the Zen gardens of Asia. These woodland gardens need little or no embellishment, but a few azaleas or Chinese dogwoods will not look amiss amongst the natives.

50

Gardening

City gardens make community, but they can also
be havens as deep as any rural fastness. The tiniest
space can be transformed into a dripping grotto,
cool with moss and loud with the splash of water.
Tiny side yards can become bowers of roses and
jasmine, screened from neighbors by flowering
shrubs and vine-laden trellises.

in Small Spaces

Simple but abundant planting transforms this narrow walkway into a lush little garden. A small recirculating fountain mounted on the house wall adds water music. A sculpted mirror brings in reflected light, expanding the apparent space through visual suggestion.

RELAXATION IS THE CRUX of the tiny garden. Many are little more than enchanting places to sit and drink in the scent of growing things. Some are entirely open to view, while others share glimpses of their growing richness with the neighborhood while retaining privacy for the owner. Enclosing fences, trellises, or walls screen the inner garden and make a structural framework for outer plantings that offer refreshment to the public. ❧ Pocket-handkerchief gardens are usually urban, made where space is at a premium. Interestingly, well-designed gardens can expand our sense of space. Plant lovers can coax a narrow city lot to hold at least six acres' worth of plants. Discovering miniature green havens squeezed between looming buildings, our spirits enlarge. ❧ Tiny gardens may be found on houseboats, sidewalk strips, or narrow condo patios. Some perch precariously on balconies high above crowded streets. Others spill out from diminutive yards, reaching past fence and gate to greet passersby. A few occur in highly unlikely places. The tiny garden below was carved out of the heart of a blackberry patch. A simple oval of grass fills its living green walls. Just big enough to swing a hammock and play toddler catch, this lilliputian space offers recreation and relaxation for a young family.

Northwest Rock Gardens

MOUNTAINS THROUGHOUT this territory are rich in natural rock gardens that inspire regional gardeners to thoughtful emulation. Sprawling mats and tight buns, spreading creepers and snaking crawlers drip from every stony surface. Vertical plantings spill like living water, shaped by the rocks that punctuate their textured tapestries. Blooming in serial sequences, these natural gardens are now a haze of blue, now rosy, now a golden sea of yellow and white. Even in autumn, the tawny tufts and mounds maintain their severe elegance of form. Winter softens both line and tint, but when not hidden by snow, the subtle coloration of seed head and leaf glows like old gilding against grey gravel and silver frost. ❡ The rocks themselves may be jutting and irregular or rounded and smoothed by the slow passage of glaciers. Recently it has become more eco-cool to use artificial rocks than real ones, because the latter are often "mined" illegally from parks and wilderness areas. Northern California artist Harlan Hand sculpts concrete into steps, troughs, containers, and waterways that suggest the natural stone gardens of the high Sierra. Not intended to be fake rocks, they simply evoke the real thing with their strength and simplicity of line.

54

Colorist Trends

CASCADIA COLORISTS are outgrowing the imitation of traditional styles, developing instead a rooted regional aesthetic. We now explore color work with fascination and curiosity, less concerned with the reactions of traditionalists than with eliciting delight from garden visitors and ourselves. Growing maturity brings the recognition that any rules that dictate right relationship are subject to personal interpretation. *J* Near Seattle, extensive mixed borders created by the Northwest Perennial Alliance at the Bellevue Botanical Garden brilliantly demonstrate these new directions. Within them, a shifting maze of plants suggests the depth and layering found in the nearby woods. Marvelous color themes and sequences develop before your eyes. Walk one way and watch white, soft pinks, and lavenders warm to buttery yellows, warm reds, and plummy blues. Reverse your course and those pinks deepen to rose, gentled by creamy or silvery foliage variegation. Move past an arching wing of shrubs and suddenly you are in the torrid tropics. Volcanic reds and ember oranges sizzle alongside electric blues, their heat muted by smoldering bronze, ashen silvers, and murky purples. *J* Though the border is often bright with bloom, much of the color work relies on leaves rather than flowers. The plantings offer an enticing sampler of foliage types, demonstrating combinations based on unusual shapes, textures, and colors. The result is a wide range of colorist effects, running from subtle to sumptuous.

Regional gardeners have distinct advantages when it comes to color work. Subdued by clouds or mist, our diffused light allows us to explore subtleties of color that burn out beneath hotter suns and bluer skies. Timidly tasteful pastels can easily be enriched by extending the palette in both directions, adding strong, clear tints tempered with white and deep, heavy tones muted with black. Pewtery light lends luster to both high and low notes, bringing out unsuspected depths in pale colors and awakening highlights in dim ones.

Artful Gardens

NORTHWEST ARTISTS are in the vanguard of contemporary garden artwork, creating a dazzling, complex body of work that embraces risk and refuses solemnity. Some borrow the vivid palette of folk art, employing all the colors found in the garden. While many contemporary garden sculptures are stained in the restrained, "natural" tints of sand and rock, others boast the singing colors of erupting volcanoes or flaunting jungle flowers. ℐ Some of the most exciting garden pieces look as if they had grown in place, rising like fanciful extensions of the garden that birthed them. Often, the garden did birth them. Some of my favorite gardens are those that serve as both studio and gallery for working artists. In them, the eros of work spills over into the pleasure of admiration. Raw materials often spill into the garden as well. Finished pieces overlap the incipience of unworked wood and stone, concrete and clay, metal and glass. Flats of new plants nestle companionably beside bags of cement or bins of mosaic tesserae. ℐ Not surprisingly, art created in such fertile settings fits more organically into gardens than do antiquities. Where classical sculpture dominates plants, plants frame and define contemporary pieces, even as their potent shapes and colors add strength and definition to the floral backdrop. Traditional works were intended to emphasize the differences rather than the connections between humans and nature. To the old school, it was important for man to distance himself from nature. As modern

culture stretches toward new definition, it seems increasingly desirable to seek and nurture human connectedness with the natural world. There is no higher art than this, and no better place to begin that search than in the garden.

Northwest

Garden Whimsy

WHERE GARDEN ART tends to be formal or serious in intention, garden whimsy introduces an element of playfulness. Like visual puns, whimsical arrangements showcase oddities and delicious absurdities. Contrived or serendipitous, successful whimsy evokes a shock of delight from viewers. More personal than universal, good whimsy is nonetheless universally engaging. Its immediacy gives it instant appeal, yet good whimsy may find a lingering home in our memory, its power to amuse remaining fresh long after its setting or circumstances have faded. ❡ For garden artists, whimsical experimentation often leads past the safe and known to untried territory. Conventional garden art can rarely be considered fun, yet wit is the soul of whimsy. Joyful self-expression tempered by humor, this liveliest of arts offers a way to explore the outer perimeters of a genre. Stretching accepted limits, taking risks without fear of failure, whimsy teaches by poking good-natured fun at strictures. Those who know themselves to be mistress or master of a certain style can further exercise their abilities in playing with its conventions. Where fastidious plans, rigidly carried out, leave no room for happy accidents, whimsy is a powerful plea for the spontaneous. ❡ More than two centuries ago, Horace Walpole, himself an ardent gardener, invented the term "serendipity" to describe the captivating result of a chance juxtaposition of objects and plants. In the garden, the natural and often short-lived occurrence of whimsical partnerings similarly encourages our appreciation for unsought grace. The best of them remind us to value the fleeting and fanciful as deeply as the deliberate.

A cheerfully painted tub treats the visitor to the idea of outdoor bathing amid a garden of ecstatically wriggling sculptures and wind-swung flowers. Even if we don't take the plunge ourselves, the very thought is emotionally freeing, as refreshing as a mental rinse with conceptual water.

61

The Gardening Year

IN THIS BOUNTIFUL REGION, the garden year ebbs and flows but never fully stops. Gardeners who want respite can certainly take it, for winter comes even to its southernmost counties. However, the hardy can pursue both active chores and contemplative pleasures in any season. The garden year differs from the ordinary calendar, dividing itself into six natural seasons. Spring glides into early summer. High summer mellows into autumn. Early winter slumps into late winter, which awakens into spring. Each slips so seamlessly into the next that the divisions are subtle. Cascadia gardeners learn to sense them by the smell of the wind, the look of a leaf. Yesterday, it was still summer, time to relax. Today, fall is in the air and a dozen dormant projects are afoot. *J* To make the most of the long garden year, we need to create places to be out of doors in all seasons. Most of us have already realized the need for a comfortable seat or two, but usually these are placed for optimal summer use. When we look past

the obvious need for a sunbathing spot or a shady retreat, we expand our sense of the garden as a place to inhabit. A sheltered bench placed where winter sun lingers longest invites us to take warming cups of tea into the garden even in January. Any place that's enclosed above but open on three sides encourages us to appreciate the scents and sounds of rain in the garden. Draped with evergreen vines and sheltered by shrubs, a covered arbor, an unused garage, or a tiny side porch becomes a viewing platform where the refreshment of rainfall can be savored in comfort.

If we are to live as well as work in our gardens, we need places to get cozy. Most garden seats are designed to please the eye but leave the body less than delighted. No matter how intent the mind, it is difficult to achieve a properly meditative spirit when the flesh is suffering. One of my favorite gardeners insists she can fully admire a garden only when horizontal. Her own tiny garden overflows with plants, yet there is always room for a cushy chaise longue.

January

JANUARY'S SHORT, DARK days are for dreams. In January, we know that this year will be different. January is the time of promise, the hour of resolution. When the New Year opens frosty, gardeners pass the long evenings in assessment, thinking about the past with an eye to the future. We plan new garden acquisitions, choose new companions for favorite plants, invent new relationships to revive. *❧* If you have no winter garden yet, find a sunny spot in a sheltered corner where you can take tea and soak up whatever warmth is on offer. A south-facing bank, mossy with thyme, makes a fragrant seat on a soft winter's day. Here, January thaws will coax the first snowdrops into timid bloom and open the silken silver catkins on native Scouler willow (*Salix scouleriana*) a good month ahead of ornamental garden varieties. The stiff-fingered twigs of winter jasmine (*Jasminum nudiflorum*) are spangled with starry golden trumpets. Creamy buds of fernleaf clematis (*Clematis cirrhosa* var. *balearica*) are swelling like tiny balloons, opening into creamy, freckled bells with a faint scent of primulas. Chinese witch hazel (*Hamamelis mollis*) and wintersweet (*Chimonanthus praecox*) offer more intense fragrance, and the first bees bumble sleepily about them, thirsty for the taste of spring.

This season of change is a good one in which to begin exploring the ways to enrich our winter gardens. Though the year may be closing in, the garden need not die with it. Indeed, it never really does, for imperceptible changes are occurring every day, from the winter solstice on into spring. If we remain alive to the garden's subtle alterations during the darkest days, we are ourselves renewed in its renewal.

February

SOFT FEBRUARY DAYS are perfect for garden tidying, clearing away the old to make room for the new. Though usually sodden, the garden feels more cheerful each week. The warm chinook melts away any ice or frost and the softening ground is beginning to release the enticing fragrance of spring. The beds are full of twittering birds feeding companionably on the seed heads of spent perennials. Robins and thrushes poke about amongst the moldering leaves, eager for early worms. *❦* As we scatter manure on the wakening borders, we find gaps where plants have exchanged their garden home for a heavenly address. If we bide our time, seedlings of plants better suited to that situation will arrive unbidden, filling the holes without effort on our part. If we don't want to wait, those empty places offer chances to experiment with new plants. Wherever losses have occurred, it's always wise to re-work the soil, digging deeply and adding amendments. Break up any big lumps of clay, and refresh sandy soils with earthy compost. This makes a more inviting home for the next inhabitant, which might be convinced to tarry a little longer. *❦* In February, the wise move slowly, pulling away last year's withered growth but replacing protective mulch. Where this has worn thin, layer on aged manure and compost, snugging those tender young shoots in a fresh blanket, just in case. Some people find this chore distasteful, but for most gardeners, manure is magical stuff, itself an alchemical conversion of basic nourishment into garden gold, which in turn converts tilth-poor ground into rich soil with a lovely texture.

Gardeners are reminded every year of an ancient truth: the garden begins in manure and ends in compost. That cycle—and recycle—is always present for us. The processes of spreading manure or turning weary garden salvage into compost remind us that no end is really The End; each one is just an ending, and all endings are doorways to new beginnings.

March

If equinoctial weather is notoriously quixotic everywhere, spring in Cascadia is memorable for extremism. Tumbles of tattered clouds keep us indoors until a burst of sunshine encourages a quick weeding session. For a golden moment, the wet grass steams with the gentle breath of mother earth. In no time, spatters of freezing rain announce the arrival of hail, which bangs against the windows and pelts the emerging garden with white marbles. Ah, spring.

BY MARCH, SPRING has broken winter's chains. Bulbs are blooming in earnest, accompanied by great ranks of early perennial companions. Dapple-leaved lungworts (*Pulmonaria* spp.) sprout clustered florets in pink or blue or white. Delicate, dancing epimediums are abob with flowers balancing like birds on a wire above elegant leaves sheened with bronze. Glossy peony shoots, glazed black or wine red, rise amid ruffles of bright-faced primroses. As our tidying hands disturb tangles of old leaves amid the beds, fragrant violets release wafts of their sweet, soapy scent on the warming air. ¶ Soon after the vernal equinox, lilac leaves split their sheaths and we can sow sweet or edible peas. When pudgy Dutch crocus bloom, sow radishes, celery, and mustard greens and plant asparagus. Border daffodils signal time to plant Spanish onions, early potatoes, and midseason broccoli. When apple leaves appear, sow spinach and parsley, scallions and carrots, lettuce and beets. This is also the right time to start tomatoes, but keep these tropical beauties indoors a while longer; they won't be able to deal with the vagaries of our stimulating Cascadia weather until the cow parsley (*Heracleum lanatum*) blooms along the roadside.

69

April

T. S. ELIOT CALLED April "the cruelest month." First, a meltingly mellow day speaks promisingly of summer. The next day, we awaken to the sodden rags of winter. If such teasing makes gardening hard to schedule, at least the plants appreciate it, for sunny days wake up dormant crowns, while rainy ones promote root growth. Around these parts, where April is also the Month of Acquisition, inclement weather means it's buying time again. Gardeners do their share of economy boosting by buying plants in bulk. Never in a spirit of greed, of course, but purely scientific inquiry requires us to experience as many plants as possible. ¶ Fairness suggests that we divide our patronage between local garden centers and regional catalog nurseries. Since each has its strength, it makes sense to buy liberally of the best all have to offer. Look to plant supermarkets for reasonably priced basics like hedge plants, border roses, ornamental vines, or culinary herbs. Small specialty nurseries go narrower but deeper, supplying select lines of uncommon plants and common ones in unusual variety. With such, we broaden our artistic palettes and make our gardens more distinctive. Catalog nurseries may specialize still further, offering only the choicest Japanese maples or species rhododendrons or the latest in horticulturally hot perennials. By shopping around, we not only gladden the hearts of hard-working nurseryfolk but also greatly enrich our gardens.

Since late winter, the fruit trees have been blooming in quick succession, first plum and cherry, then apple, peach, and pear. Young and upright or gnarled with age, they foam with flowers, looming against the landscape like thunderheads. In April, cherry blossom falls like fragrant snow, lapping in pools of pale color at the base of each trunk. In gardens and orchards, parks and parking lots, petals drift into piles like seawrack, their spent beauty jumbled into tired heaps of pink and rose and alabaster.

May

Excess is almost always a good thing in a garden. Indeed, generally speaking, excess is the gardener's best friend. Especially in the early years of a garden, excess makes for abundance and generosity. However, unless kept in check, it becomes clutter, obscuring the very qualities we wanted to emphasize. While it takes work to keep a full garden in balance, the rewards are many and deeply satisfying. Disciplined editing brings renewal, clarifying the design beneath the muddle. Then, each plant can again be seen both for itself and in solid relationship to the living community around it.

MAY IS THE MONTH of rhododendrons and species roses and drooping, heavy-headed peonies, yet its splendid excess culminates only when garden foliage reaches the peak of perfection. As the month matures, burgeoning border plants knit themselves together to create the intricate green tapestry of summer. Fabulous as May's flowers are, most are fleeting indeed, so it behooves us to choose early bloomers with care, giving preference to those with continuing charms extending over several seasons. ❦ Like rhododendrons, peonies are best chosen as whole plants. Indeed, these stout perennials often appear as solidly structural as shrubs, supporting flimsier creatures with their comforting bulk. Peonies are among the briefest bloomers, yet many boast extraordinary seedpods that split to reveal rosy linings and glistening black seeds. Peony foliage presents the gardener with a delightful diversity of form and texture, from feathery and finely cut to broad, leathery, and boldly lobed. In late winter, fat peony shoots emerge from the chilly earth lustrously lacquered in ruby or burgundy or black, their tints especially potent when Japanese species are involved in their breeding. In Cascadia, both species and garden forms frequently exchange their deep summer greenery for hot autumnal hues of orange and scarlet, brass and old gold.

June

DURING THE LONG DAYS and short nights around the summer solstice, June's astonishing floral bounty illuminates the tender, lingering twilights. The borders billow with plump peonies and soaring delphiniums. All is freshness, sumptuous scent, and glowing light. Roses lace the old fruit trees in exuberant swags, spilling in perfumed curtains at the border back. The Austin roses open tapered, elegant buds into fragrant extravaganzas of silk crêpe and georgette. Old roses, hooped and crinolined, heap their cascading skirts with bud and blossom, all enriching the air with their sweet breath. *¶* June is prime blossom time in many gardens, but much of its glory is brief. Like all climaxes, this one begins to slide downhill almost the minute we notice

it. Happily, that peak experience can be extended through frequent, light grooming. Take your first cup of coffee into the garden each morning, trusty Felco pruners in hand, and snip away spent flowers and yellowed foliage. Even with daily intervention, however, by month's end gardens that have been performing nonstop are getting a bit tired and will benefit from judicious tidying. Avoid major make-overs, for nothing can plunge your garden straight from peak to valley faster. June's great grooming session is more of a refresher, a process of feeding and thinning to keep the garden looking great as the heat comes on.

In June, carefully thin areas where growth is beginning to look rank rather than refined. With vigorous hardy geraniums, achilleas, or taller veronicas, you may remove up to a third of the shoots entirely, cutting back any remaining stems that straggle. Leggy phlox and lanky asters can be pinched back, also by a third. The result will be shapely, well-furnished plants that bloom abundantly and with lasting vigor.

July

High-summer shearing rejuvenates sprawling catmints (*Nepeta* spp.) that bloomed themselves out in June. Cut back by half, they refurbish quickly, often reblooming several times. Woody herbs like lavender and sage can also be lightly trimmed now to encourage bushiness.

Both culinary and ornamental herbs perform splendidly in pots, which can decorate less than ideal places. New plants need regular water, of course, but once established and showing new growth, most herbs will happily take all the sun they can get. Indeed, woody Mediterranean natives like sage and rosemary, lavender and thyme love hot spots and dry soils, so reflected heat off neighboring apartments or the street leaves them lush rather than limp.

THE BUILDING HEAT of July deepens the garden's living perfume, adding the bracing bite of aromatic herbs to June's flowery blend. Astringent lavender, brisk rosemary, and pungent artemisias provide a stimulating counterbalance to the rather cloying midsummer fragrances of lilies and tuberoses, honeysuckle and jasmine, datura and mock orange. Certain herbal scents, notably spearmint and lemon verbena, lift weary spirits instantly. The firm shapes and bold textures of evergreen herbs are similarly refreshing to gardens battered by heat, for herbs revel in summer sun. ❧ Though herb gardens have their charm, many herbs are ornamental enough to win places in mixed borders. Columnar 'Tuscan Blue' rosemary and upright lavenders like 'Fred Boutin' make living sculpture amid flurries of fine-leaved perennials. Herb foliage boasts an astonishing variety of form and color, from the wiry lace of black chervil, *Anthriscus sylvestris* 'Ravenswing', to the broadly lobed, sea-green leaves of burgundy-blossomed *Angelica gigas*. Pewtery artemisias and silvery sages temper the hard, hot reds and oranges of summer, as do sleek mounds of steel-blue rues and ruffled golden oreganos.

August

DURING THE DOG DAYS of high summer, the smoldering, passionate colors come into their own. In spring and early summer, when all is freshness and new beginnings, heavy, smoky colors can seem sulky, out of sympathy with the season. Now the dark tones sing out, brought to perfection by heat and the potent light of an August afternoon. Beside them, creams and silvers glimmer like stones in moonlight, making an understated contrast to the explosive qualities of volcanic reds and ember oranges. ❧ A little of this intensity goes a long way, however. In a large garden, a series of small but vibrant combinations can be judiciously arranged to lighten solid masses of foliage where early bloomers have made their bow and left the stage. In a very small garden, a single flaming floral eruption might be the culmination of a long run of gentler tints of rose and cream. Let mauve build to rose and ruby, lavender to murky purples, slate and steel to midnight and thundercloud. The effect will be both delicate and powerful, as befits this sultry, sensuous season.

August's golden moon spills liquid light over the garden, washing lawns and borders in silver-gilt. This is the magic moment for white gardens, for when deep tones recede to invisibility, reflected moonlight brings pale flowers to prominence. Not just whites, but creams and chalky yellows, clear lavenders and certain soft blues phosphoresce mysteriously both at twilight and under the stars. On warm August nights, heady fragrances saturate the still air. Pots of night-scented stocks and *Nicotiana alata* 'Fragrant Cloud', honeysuckle and strongly perfumed lilies will create an intensely romantic atmosphere if placed where you sit outside at night.

September

Most gardens peak in spring and summer. Transforming them into places with year-round presence takes time and thought as well as experience. It begins with observation, both at home and elsewhere. As we work in our own gardens, we can identify places that work and places that need help. When we visit gardens or nurseries, we can keep notes about plants that look great when our gardens are less well-stocked. Gradually, we develop lists of possibilities to try, and ideas for combining them in graceful, effective vignettes that will suit our own gardens.

THE SEPTEMBER GARDEN is still fairly full, but even where late bloomers are plentiful, the overall impression is of harvest rather than hope. Globe thistles are thick with greedy goldfinches, goldenrods are turning buff and tan, and the sunflowers are ripening their glossy, striped seeds. As you walk through the garden in the early morning, it's clear that summer is on the wane. The morning mist is thicker and more golden. The spiderwebs are tattered and bedraggled. The ruffling wind tosses yellowing leaves into your coffee cup. Geese are winging overhead and early apples tumble from the trees, decorating the grass with globes of green and gold and rosy red. However, it isn't time to toss in the trowel yet. Though most gardens are looking decidedly worse for wear, autumn chores should be inspired by renewal rather than retreat. If summer's charms are dwindling rapidly, those of fall are yet to come, and beyond them lie those of winter. We tidy the borders lightly, making the most of anything that remains attractive. While we work, we can also be assessing what's left. With winter on the way, we want any plants that have off-season beauties to look presentable. To this end, we first remove unsightly leftovers, then consider improvements. What might we offer them in the way of supportive companions? Where can a single strong plant be expanded into an off-season vignette? Over time, such thoughts lead to actions that continually enrich the garden.

81

$\mathit{October}$

IF EVER THERE WAS a month designed expressly for gardeners, it must be a sunny October. Fall flowers are flickering out, yet foliage displays remain extravagant, with flaming maples vying for attention with burning bush (*Euonymus alata*), sunset-colored forsythia, and ember-red fothergillas—compact, shrubby witch hazel relatives that ignite in fall. Warm Octobers make seasonal chores like dividing perennials and planting shrubs a positive delight. ❦ Autumn planting is generally reckoned

to mean plugging in bulbs rather than plants. However, fall is a splendid time to establish those bargain perennials that languish in half-empty nurseries. They may look a bit worse for wear, but kindly planted and generously mulched, most will rebound with elan. Most shrubs and trees appreciate fall planting as well. Though the heat of summer is tempered, enough warmth remains in the soil that root growth continues till frost. Misty mornings and heavy dews help to keep transplants from drying out, and cooling breezes take the edge off the heat of the afternoon sun. In dry years, it's vital to keep newly planted roots moist as they ready themselves for winter, but you don't want to encourage new top growth by feeding new plantings anything stronger than compost and aged manure.

Garden newcomers are vulnerable to winter frosts as well as drought, so mulch them deeply before temperatures plummet. To fend off hungry mice seeking cozy winter abodes, scatter a handful of smelly, naphtha-based mothballs or flakes in with the mulch material. Shredded or chopped leaves also provide terrific insulation, but don't use whole leaves unless they are fine-textured and small. Little birch or hawthorn leaves are fine, but bigleaf maple or big oak leaves simply form dense, slippery mats that smother rather than protect the plants.

November

Autumn's fading splendors have a tattered opulence that only the heartless could prune away. Left in place, aging hydrangea heads billow like seafoam above drooping, gilded leaves. Such magnificence makes a splendid backdrop for the last of the autumn crocus and the glittering satin-pink ribbons of *Nerine bowdenii,* emerging glorious from a haze of reblooming catmint and wreaths of purple grape, or elegantly wrapped in a silvery boa of immortelle, *Helichrysum petiolare.*

BY NOVEMBER, autumn has arrived in earnest, and its fitful rains and sudden, swirling winds are making colorful havoc in the garden. Like the poet Andrew Marvell, I find this sweet disarray entrancing, perhaps all the more because it is utterly beyond any control of the gardener. As we tidy away the ruins of summer or plant new beds with hopeful anticipation, the playful wind releases a hundred armloads of bright leaves in fearless free fall and our hearts are lifted up by their carefree dance. Who can help feeling festive when border and lawn are strewn again and again with such glorious foliar confetti. *¶* Amid the swirling leaves, a handful of perennials cheerfully linger despite the threat of frost. Scrambling, bright-eyed *Geranium wallichianum* 'Buxton's Blue' throws long arms companionably about its neighbors. Mottled and lacy, its leaves turn autumnal red-gold, the perfect foil for its white-throated, sky-blue flowers. Tall spikes of obedient plant *Physostegia virginiana* 'Variegata' remain rosy above long leaves heavily streaked with cream, pink, and sage. Strawberry-leaved *Potentilla nepalensis* 'Miss Willmott' is heavy with rebloom, its black-eyed, salmon-pink flowers glowing hotly against a fiery smoke bush, *Cotinus coggygria* 'Velvet Cloak'.

December

AS THE JUICE and joy of summer drains slowly away, the garden is left with a new beauty, one that requires educated eyes to appreciate. Bronzed and brown, slumping in graceful fatigue, perennials drift off to their gentle winter sleep. Tumbling in slow motion, pulled by the inexorable tug of gravity toward the embrace of mother earth, they slide into the next stage in the endless cycle of change and decay. ❧ This twilight of the garden has a magic of its own, touched both with melancholy and with the promise of renewal. By December, the garden's bones are revealed and strengths of design or lapses of balance are laid bare. Should strengths be in short supply, we can amuse ourselves all winter by dreaming up ways to increase structural elements, introduce more powerful off-season performers, and create more fundamentally harmonious arrangements of our plants. ❧ Cascadia's gentle winters allow adventurous gardeners to develop winter vignettes that increase in power and drama as the year wanes. Nursery shopping in winter introduces us to an abundance of winter performers, excitingly varied in form, texture, color, and habit. Arrange your favorites in compatible groups to create clustered pockets of winter beauty throughout the garden.

The fundamentals of garden design count for a great deal in winter. Without the distraction of flowers and foliage, structural elements like trelliswork and columns, seats and stairs gain visual importance. Too often, however, what is revealed by winter's knife is simply framework. Structural plants keep the garden alive in winter. If perennials melt to mush beneath rain or snow, broad-leaved evergreens come into their own.

Futures

CASCADIA MUST BE the most exciting place in the world to be gardening right now. This is the epicenter of contemporary garden design, for nowhere is more experimentation, exploration, and reinterpretation going on than right here in our own backyards. Though myriad styles are being developed and refined, nearly all share common ground. Overwhelmingly, we want our gardens to be healthy places, good both for people and for the earth. Increasingly, we base our gardens less on chemical intervention than on cooperative understanding, asking our plants only to fulfil their natural inclinations, and placing them where those inclinations accord with our own desires. ❧ A true garden is more than a bunch of plants stuck in a border. Our gardens are extensions of ourselves, living expressions of taste and joy. They are the concrete aspect of our relationship with plants. For most of us, the garden is a haven, the place where we find comfort. We work in the good soil, weeding and planting, and peace seeps up through our fingers as we touch the earth. A garden can be as small as a window box and still deliver an astonishing amount of pleasure. ❧ Gardening is often compared with addiction because of the way it takes over and saturates our lives. It has qualities we associate with addiction, notably the constant longing for more, yet I think our confused culture readily confounds addiction's hunger with the spiritual thirst for the real. Where addiction craves oblivion, the gardener's yearning is for life. Gardening is an essentially healthy activity, with healing and well-being as its fruits. That gardening feels like a spiritual pursuit should not be surprising, for the rites and rituals of the garden year are those of the first churches, as ancient as agriculture, as ancient perhaps as humanity. Spring sowing and fall harvest, fertility and fullness, birth and death put us in electrically genuine connection with the cycles of altering reality that make the natural year. ❧ I believe the gardens of the future will reflect the ancient truth that when we are in right relationship with our gardens, we are in right relationship to the earthly environment and to ourselves.

Books for Further Reading

CASCADIA IS BLESSED not only in climate and soil but in an abundance of regional garden writers. Their direct, local experience is invaluable to newcomers, whose own gardening lessons may have been learned in very different circumstances. Their works are also of enormous benefit to longtime residents who are branching out in new directions or simply want to enjoy the luxury of reading about gardens similar to their own. ❧ Some books are indispensable here, notably the *Sunset Western Garden Book*. This book has been evolving through new editions for over forty years. Like its cousin, *Sunset* magazine, the *Western Garden Book* addresses Cascadia issues as a matter of course. Sunset Publishing produces a whole slew of smaller handbooks on dozens of topics from water gardening to installing your own garden deck, all designed specifically for western gardeners. ❧ Several other regional publishers have made sterling contributions to Cascadia garden writing. Sasquatch Books has made a point of keeping numerous Northwestern classics in print, updating them periodically. It also produces the Cascadia Gardening Series of handbooks (individually listed here). Timber Press in Portland supports regional gardeners by co-publishing quantities of English and European books that apply more directly to Cascadia gardens than do those spawned along the Eastern seaboard, where so many American garden books originate. Best of all, the genre is rapidly growing as regional gardeners realize the treasury of knowledge and experience they represent and begin to share it in words and pictures.

Barton, Barbara. *Gardening by Mail: A Source Book.* Boston: Houghton-Mifflin, 1994.

Colebrook, Binda. *Winter Gardening in the Maritime Northwest.* Seattle: Sasquatch Books, 1989.

Feeney, Stephanie. *The Northwest Gardener's Resource Directory.* Cedarcroft Press, 1995.

Gordon, George David. *Field Guide to the Slug.* Seattle: Sasquatch Books, 1994.

Grant, John and Carol L. Grant. *Trees and Shrubs for Pacific Northwest Gardens.* Portland: Timber Press, 1990.

Hart, Rhonda M. *North Coast Roses* (Cascadia Gardening Series). Seattle: Sasquatch Books, 1993.

Hinkley, Daniel. *Winter Ornamentals* (Cascadia Gardening Series). Seattle: Sasquatch Books, 1993.

Kennedy, Des. *Crazy About Gardening.* Seattle: Alaska Northwest Books, 1994.

———. *Nature's Outcasts: A New Look at Living Things We Love to Hate.* Pownal, Vermont: Garden Way, 1993.

Kruckeberg, Arthur. *Gardening with Native Plants of the Pacific Northwest.* Seattle and London: University of Washington Press, 1995.

Lovejoy, Ann. *The American Mixed Border.* New York: Macmillan Publishing, 1993.

———. *The Border in Bloom.* Seattle: Sasquatch Books, 1990.

———. *Fragrance in Bloom.* Seattle: Sasquatch Books, 1996.

———. *Further Along the Garden Path.* New York: Macmillan Publishing, 1995.

———. *Seasonal Bulbs* (Cascadia Gardening Series). Seattle: Sasquatch Books, 1995.

———. *Three Years in Bloom.* Seattle: Sasquatch Books, 1991.

———. *The Year in Bloom.* Seattle: Sasquatch Books, 1987.

Oakley, Myrna. *Public & Private Gardens of the Northwest.* Wilsonville, Oregon: Beautiful America Publishing Company, 1990.

Preus, Mary. *Growing Herbs.* (Cascadia Gardening Series). Seattle: Sasquatch Books, 1994.

Schenk, George. *The Complete Shade Gardener.* Boston: Houghton Mifflin, 1984.

Solomon, Steve. *Growing Vegetables West of the Cascades.* Seattle: Sasquatch Books, 1989.

———. *Organic Gardening West of the Cascades.* Seattle: Pacific Search Press, 1981.

———. *Water-Wise Vegetables* (Cascadia Gardening Series). Seattle: Sasquatch Books, 1993.

Sunset Western Garden Annual, 1996, Menlo Park: Sunset Books, 1996.

Tarrant, David. *David Tarrant's Pacific Gardening Guide.* Portland: Whitecap Books, 1990.

Whitner, Jan K. *Garden Touring in the Pacific Northwest.* Seattle: Alaska Northwest Books, 1993.

———. *Northwest Garden Style, Ideas, Designs, and Methods for the Creative Gardener.* Seattle: Sasquatch Books, 1996.

Acknowledgments

The author and the photographer heartily thank the dozens of gardeners all over Cascadia who so generously invited us into their gardens and homes. Your artistry, your hard work, your thoughtful experimentation, and your affectionate delight in plants are the inspiration for this book.
Floreat Cascadia!

—A. L.

To travel Cascadia focusing on images for this book has been an eye-opening delight for me. To be able to visit gardens as spectacular as their gardeners who hoe and hone their land into places of fine art has been truly inspiring. *❧* To witness the beauty and balance that occurs when we work and play from the deep connection with earth has renewed my optimism that we folks can protect and restore the intended richness and integrity of our planet. *❧* I wish to extend my appreciation to Ann Lovejoy for her dedication to artful gardening and her invitation to join her in the creation of this book. *❧* To Sasquatch Books for their wise valuing of the beauty of Cascadia and their professional style and expertise. *❧* To my husband Rich, who is my constant help mate, artistically, technically, and lovingly. *❧* To my circle sisters and their unconditional love. *❧* To the incredible earth-friendly gardeners who as they awaken to their own beauty and blessings are making a difference in our world: Sally Anderson, Leslie Beach, Kluane Bickerton, Linda J. Cochran, Marcia Donahue, Elizabeth England, Sonny Q. Garcia, Cora L. Gardiner, Bobbie Garthwaite and Joseph Sullivan, Harlan J. Hand, Cyril Hume, Judith Lawrence, David Lewis and George Little, Eileen Makinson, Lindsay R. Smith, Jack Todds, Gayle M. Villarreal, and Bill and June Willard. *❧* Thanks also to: Bellevue Botanical Gardens, The Butchart Gardens, Horticulture Centre of the Pacific, Kubota Gardens, Sutter Home Wines, A & D Peony and Perennial Nursery (Snohomish, Washington), Mosswood Perennials (Victoria, British Columbia), The Country Store (Vashon Island, Washington), The Water Garden (Yountville, California), Schreiner's Gardens (Salem, Oregon), and VanDusen Botanical Garden (Vancouver, British Columbia). *❧* And to Great Mystery for always being here, there, and everywhere.

—S. L. R.

About the Authors

ANN LOVEJOY is the author of *The Year in Bloom*, *The Border in Bloom*, *The American Mixed Border*, *Fragrance in Bloom*, and *Further Along the Garden Path*. She is the recipient of the American Horticultural Society Writing Award, and her articles appear in *Horticulture*, *The Seattle Post-Intelligencer*, and *House & Garden*, among others. She lives on Bainbridge Island, Washington.

SANDRA LEE REHA runs Nature's Elegance Gallery with her husband, Rich Reha. They are known throughout the Northwest and the West for their portraits of florals, gardens, and landscapes of nature. Sandra's work has been shown in many galleries, and she has received the yearly top five photographers' award from the Seattle Arts Commision. She lives in Bellevue, Washington. (The Internet address for Nature's Elegance Gallery is http://www.natures-elegance.com/art.)

01 00 99 98 97   5 4 3 2 1

Published by Sasquatch Books.

Printed in Hong Kong.

Distributed in Canada by Raincoast Books Ltd.

Credits:

Cover and interior design: Marquand Books, Inc.

Copy editor: Alice Copp Smith

Library of Congress Cataloging in Publication Data
Lovejoy, Ann, 1951–
    [Cascadia]
    Cascadia : Inspired Gardening in the Pacific Northwest / photography by Sandra Lee Reha.
      p.   cm.
    Includes bibliographical references.
    ISBN 1-57061-099-1
    1. Gardening—Northwest, Pacific. I. Title.
    SB453.2.N83L67 1997
    635.9'09795—dc20   97-42378

Sasquatch Books
615 Second Avenue, Suite 260
Seattle, Washington 98104
(206) 467-4301
books@sasquatchbooks.com
http://www.sasquatchbooks.com
Sasquatch Books publishes high-quality adult nonfiction and children's books related to the Northwest (Alaska to San Francisco). For more information about our titles, contact us at the address above, or view our site on the World Wide Web.